Read for a Better World™

GYMNASTICS

A First Look

PERCY LEED

GRL Consultant, Diane Craig, Certified Literacy Specialist

Lerner Publications ◆ Minneapolis

Educator Toolbox

Reading books is a great way for kids to express what they're interested in. Before reading this title, ask the reader these questions:

> What do you think this book is about? Look at the cover for clues.
>
> What do you already know about gymnastics?
>
> What do you want to learn about gymnastics?

Let's Read Together

Encourage the reader to use the pictures to understand the text.

Point out when the reader successfully sounds out a word.

Praise the reader for recognizing sight words such as *is* and *on*.

TABLE OF CONTENTS

Gymnastics

Gymnastics is a sport.
Kids of all ages do it.

You can do it at clubs.

You can do it at some schools too.

Wear clothes that are easy to move in.

Warm up first.
You should stretch.
It helps you bend.

What other sports do you warm up for?

Do tumbling on the mats.
You can jump and flip.

Some people use music.

What kind of music would you use?

Walk on the balance beam.

You can do tricks.

Older kids use the vault.

They swing on bars.

Get help from an adult. This helps keep you safe.

How else can you be safe?

Gymnastics is a fun sport!

You Connect!

Have you ever done gymnastics before?

What about gymnastics seems most fun to you?

How could you get better at gymnastics?

Social and Emotional Snapshot

Student voice is crucial to building reader confidence. Ask the reader:

What is your favorite part of this book?

What is something you learned from this book?

Did this book remind you of any sports you play?

Opportunities for social and emotional learning are everywhere. How can you connect the topic of this book to the SEL competencies below?

Responsible Decision-Making
Self-Awareness
Self-Management

Photo Glossary

balance beam

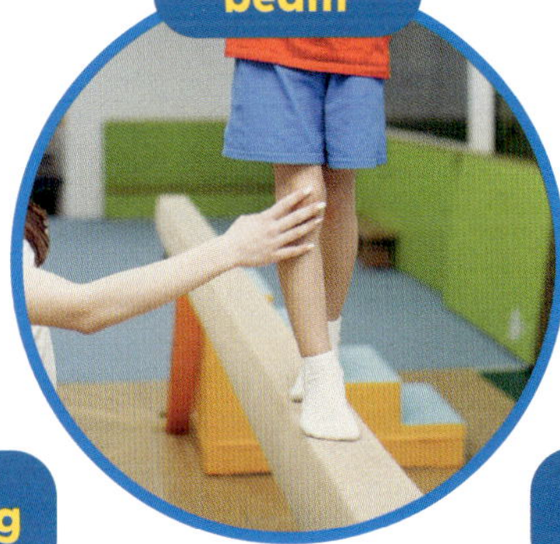

mats

tumbling

vault

Learn More

Fishman, Jon M. *Gymnastics Superstar Simone Biles*. Minneapolis: Lerner Publications, 2019.

Flynn, Sarah Wassner. *National Geographic Readers: Gymnastics (L2)*. Washington: National Geographic Kids, 2021.

Walduck, Vincent. *My Book of Gymnastics*. New York: DK Publishing, 2020.

Index

Photo Acknowledgments

The images in this book are used with the permission of: © oleg66/iStockphoto, pp. 4–5; © RichLegg/iStockphoto, p. 6; © Anatoliy Karlyuk/Shutterstock Images, p. 7; © Elena Nichizhenova/Shutterstock Images, pp. 8–9; © kool99/iStockphoto, p. 10; © Robert Kneschke/Shutterstock Images, pp. 10–11, 23 (mats); © Michael C. Gray/Shutterstock Images, pp. 12, 23 (tumbling); © PH888/Shutterstock Images, p. 13; © primipil/iStockphoto, pp. 14, 23 (balance beam); © Image Source/iStockphoto, p. 15; © Sasha Samardzija/Shutterstock Images, pp. 16, 23 (vault); © Master1305/Shutterstock Images, p. 17; © Capuski/iStockphoto, pp. 18–19; © Manaana.a/Shutterstock Images, p. 20.

Cover Photograph: © KK Tan/Shutterstock Images.

Design Elements: © Mighty Media, Inc.

Lerner Publications Company
An imprint of Lerner Publishing Group, Inc.
241 First Avenue North
Minneapolis, MN 55401 USA

For reading levels and more information, look up this title at www.lernerbooks.com.

Main body text set in Mikado a Medium.
Typeface provided by Hannes von Doehren.

Library of Congress Cataloging-in-Publication Data

Names: Leed, Percy, 1968- author.
Title: Gymnastics : a first look / Percy Leed.
Description: Minneapolis, MN : Lerner Publications, [2023] | Series: Read about sports. Read for a better world. | Includes bibliographical references and index. | Audience: Ages 5-8 | Audience: Grades K-1 | Summary: "Stretch, swing, and tumble into gymnastics. Young readers will get an exciting first glimpse of gymnastics with accessible text and fun photos"— Provided by publisher.
Identifiers: LCCN 2022011583 (print) | LCCN 2022011584 (ebook) | ISBN 9781728475714 (library binding) | ISBN 9781728479040 (paperback) | ISBN 9781728484501 (ebook)
Subjects: LCSH: Gymnastics—Juvenile literature.
Classification: LCC GV461.3 .L44 2023 (print) | LCC GV461.3 (ebook) | DDC 796.44092/2 [B]—dc23

LC record available at https://lccn.loc.gov/2022011583
LC ebook record available at https://lccn.loc.gov/2022011584

Manufactured in the United States of America
1 - CG - 12/15/22